ADVANCED DUNGEONS & DYNAMICS 365 IMPLEMENTATION GUIDE

THE WATERDEEP TRADING COMPANY PROJECT

MODULE 1: SETTING UP A CLOUD-HOSTED ENVIRONMENT FOR DYNAMICS 365

MURRAY FIFE

ISBN-13: 978-1077180307

Preface

I have been reviving an old project that started a while ago and have started up a new project blog to track the progress. Being a lifelong fan of Dungeons & Dragons, with the unfortunate problem that I cannot find anyone to play with I have decided to create a test implementation Dynamics 365 in the AD&D format just to see how it would work and if I can find some creative ways to use Dynamics 365 and chose to implement the **Waterdeep Trading Company** as an example where I can track their many legal (and not so legal) entities within Faerûn.

dync
www.dynamicscompanions.com
Dynamics Companions

- 3 -

www.blindsquirrelpublishing.com
© 2019 Blind Squirrel Publishing, LLC , All Rights Reserved

BLIND SQUIRREL
PUBLISHING

www.dynamicscompanions.com
Dynamics Companions

- 4 -

www.blindsquirrelpublishing.com
© 2019 Blind Squirrel Publishing, LLC , All Rights Reserved

BLIND SQUIRREL
PUBLISHING

Table of Contents

www.dynamicscompanions.com
Dynamics Companions

- 6 -

www.blindsquirrelpublishing.com
© 2019 Blind Squirrel Publishing, LLC , All Rights Reserved

BLIND SQUIRREL
PUBLISHING

Introduction

The **Waterdeep Trading Company** is the purveyor of all the finest adventuring supplies to travelers, rogues, wizards and clerics in all Faerûn, and are headquartered in the great city of **Waterdeep** on the **Sword Coast**.

Recently they have been experiencing a huge upswing in the traffic through their store and have realized that the old quill and scroll based financial system is not going to scale any more, and their manual supply chain management processes that they are using will not be able to handle their forecasted future demand.

As a result, they have taken the step to modernize their finance and supply chain systems and implement **Microsoft Dynamics 365** to manage all their legal (and not so legal) entities, and the following is a journal of how they set up their system, and how they tweaked the system to make it work perfectly for them.

If you want to follow along in the journey and set up your own copy of the system, then feel free.

www.dynamicscompanions.com
Dynamics Companions

- 7 -

www.blindsquirrelpublishing.com
© 2019 Blind Squirrel Publishing, LLC , All Rights Reserved

BLIND SQUIRREL
PUBLISHING

Setting up a Cloud-hosted environment for Dynamics 365

Before we can start off on our journey of setting up our new company within Dynamics 365, we need to set up a cloud-hosted environment of Dynamics 365 that we can work in.

We will do that by setting up a cloud-hosted environment within Azure, which will be funded by an Azure subscription that we have on our account.

Topics Covered

- Configuring Your Azure Subscription
- Creating a Cloud-hosted environment
- Summary

Configuring Your Azure Subscription

The first thing that we will want to do is to make sure that we have an Azure subscription that we can use to pay for the virtual machine which we will deploy to access our Dynamics 365 instance.

If we already have a subscription, then we can skip the following steps.

If we don't have an active Azure subscription though, we will want to add one to our Azure account to use later when we deploy Dynamics 365.

Topics Covered

- Getting a Free Trial Azure Subscription

- Upgrading the Free Trial to a Pay-As-You-Go Subscription

- Adding the Dynamics Deployment Service as a Contributor

- Review

Getting a Free Trial Azure Subscription

If this is the first time that you have used Azure to set up a subscription, then you are in luck, because we can take advantage of the Free Trial Subscription which will give us $200 in free azure credits that we can use for the first 30 days.

If at the end of this time we don't want to continue and convert this to a Pay-As-You-Go subscription, then we can just cancel the subscription.

Since the Cloud-hosted environment will cost a little bit of money – around $500 a month if you keep it up and running all the time, then getting a credit as we are testing this out is a great thing to take advantage of.

So, let's start off the process by signing up for a free trial subscription.

How to do it..

Step 1: Navigate to https://portal.azure.com and log in

To start off we will want to open a browser and go to the Azure Portal website.

Navigate to https://portal.azure.com and log in with the credentials that you want to use to access your Dynamics 365 Cloud-hosted environment.

Step 2: Search for Subscriptions

Next we will want to go to the Subscriptions area within the Azure Portal.

Type in **sub** into the search box in the header of the Azure Portal and that will allow us to select the **Subscriptions** service.

Step 3: Click on the Add button

This will take us to the **Subscriptions** page where we will be able to maintain all the

subscriptions that we may want to set up within Azure.

Right now, we don't have any, so we will want to add a new Subscription to our Azure account.

Click on the **Add** button.

Step 4: Click on the Sign in button

This may ask us to sign into the portal again using the credentials that we used to log into Azure in the first place to confirm that we are who we are and that someone isn't trying to sneak onto our system and set up subscriptions that we don't want.

Confirm our password for the account and click on the **Sign in** button.

Step 5: Click on the Free Trial button

This will take us to the **Add Subscription** page where we will see that we have several different options that we can choose from when we set up our subscriptions.

We will want to start off by taking advantage of the free trial offer.

Click on the **Free Trial** button.

Step 6: Enter About you details and click Next

This will take us to the Free Trial signup page within Azure.

We will start off by entering all the information that is required in the **About you** section of the sign-up page.

Fill in the account information and then click on the **Next** button.

Step 7: Enter the Identify verification by card details and click Next

This will then take us to a section where we need to verify that we are who we are by providing some credit card information.

All we need to do here is provide a valid credit card, and the associated details.

Enter in all the credit card information and the billing address before clicking on the **Next** button.

Step 8: Change the I agree and click on the Sign up button

All we need to do here is confirm that we agree to the terms and conditions and sign on up.

Toggle the **I agree** switch and set it to **Checked** and click on the **Sign up** button.

Getting a Free Trial Azure Subscription

How to do it..

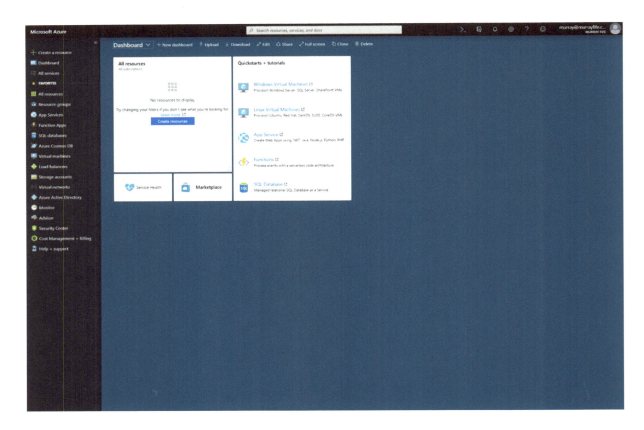

Step 1: Navigate to https://portal.azure.com and log in

To start off we will want to open a browser and go to the Azure Portal website.

To do this, just navigate to https://portal.azure.com and log in with the credentials that you want to use to access your Dynamics 365 Cloud-hosted environment.

This will take us to the Azure Portal where we will be able to start configuring our Azure subscription.

www.dynamicscompanions.com
Dynamics Companions

- 12 -

www.blindsquirrelpublishing.com
© 2019 Blind Squirrel Publishing, LLC , All Rights Reserved

BLIND SQUIRREL
PUBLISHING

Getting a Free Trial Azure Subscription

How to do it..

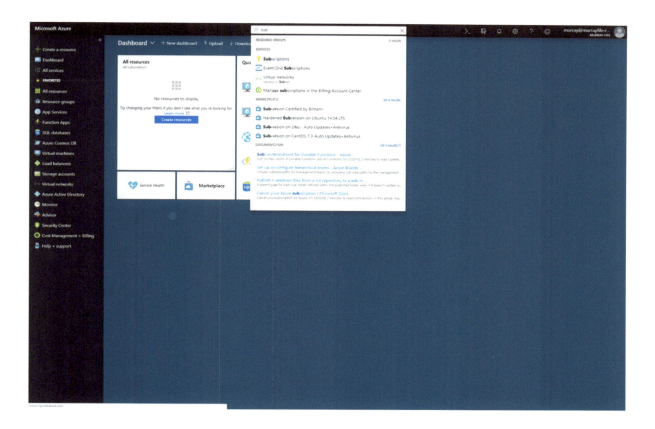

Step 2: Search for Subscriptions

Next we will want to go to the Subscriptions area within the Azure Portal.

To do this we will just type in **sub** into the search box in the header of the Azure Portal and that will allow us to select the **Subscriptions** service.

www.dynamicscompanions.com
Dynamics Companions

- 13 -

www.blindsquirrelpublishing.com
© 2019 Blind Squirrel Publishing, LLC , All Rights Reserved

BLIND SQUIRREL
PUBLISHING

Getting a Free Trial Azure Subscription

How to do it..

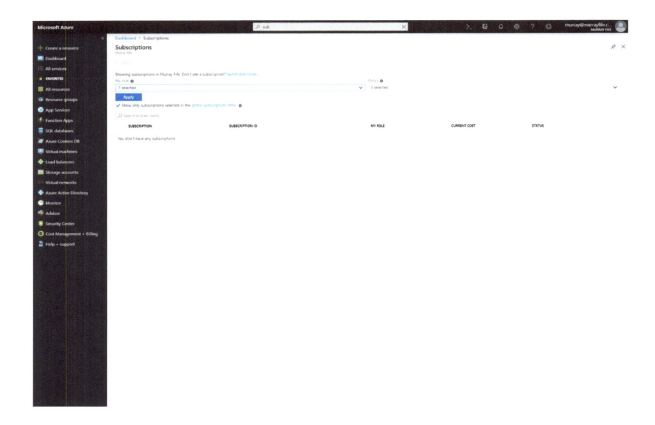

Step 3: Click on the Add button

This will take us to the **Subscriptions** page where we will be able to maintain all the subscriptions that we may want to set up within Azure.

Right now, we don't have any, so we will want to add a new Subscription to our Azure account.

To do this all we need to do is click on the **Add** button.

www.dynamicscompanions.com
Dynamics Companions

- 14 -

www.blindsquirrelpublishing.com
© 2019 Blind Squirrel Publishing, LLC , All Rights Reserved

BLIND SQUIRREL
PUBLISHING

Getting a Free Trial Azure Subscription

How to do it..

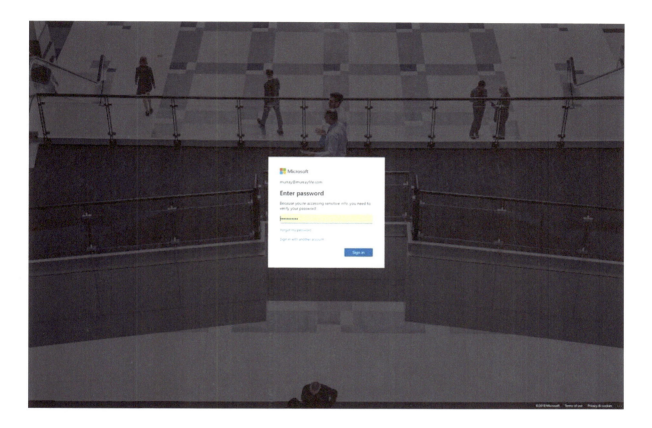

Step 4: Click on the Sign in button

This may ask us to sign into the portal again using the credentials that we used to log into Azure in the first place to confirm that we are who we are and that someone isn't trying to sneak onto our system and set up subscriptions that we don't want.

To do this just confirm our password for the account and click on the **Sign in** button.

www.dynamicscompanions.com
Dynamics Companions

- 15 -

www.blindsquirrelpublishing.com
© 2019 Blind Squirrel Publishing, LLC , All Rights Reserved

BLIND SQUIRREL
PUBLISHING

Getting a Free Trial Azure Subscription

How to do it..

Step 5: Click on the Free Trial button

This will take us to the **Add Subscription** page where we will see that we have several different options that we can choose from when we set up our subscriptions.

We will want to start off by taking advantage of the free trial offer.

To do this all we need to do is click on the **Free Trial** button.

Getting a Free Trial Azure Subscription

How to do it..

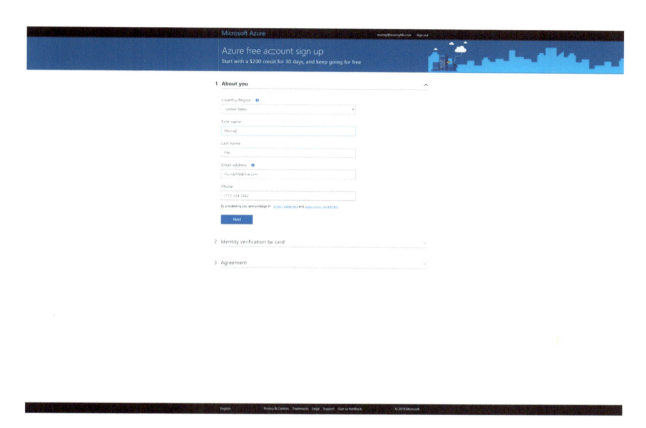

Step 6: Enter About you details and click Next

This will take us to the Free Trial signup page within Azure.

We will start off by entering all the information that is required in the **About you** section of the sign-up page.

To do this we will just fill in the account information and then click on the **Next** button.

www.dynamicscompanions.com
Dynamics Companions

- 17 -

www.blindsquirrelpublishing.com
© 2019 Blind Squirrel Publishing, LLC , All Rights Reserved

BLIND SQUIRREL
PUBLISHING

Getting a Free Trial Azure Subscription

How to do it..

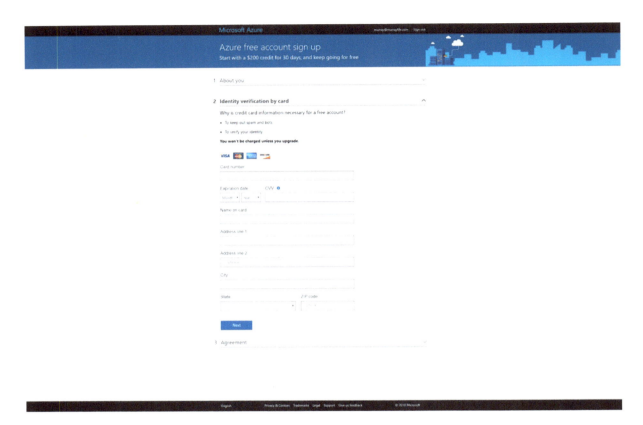

Step 7: Enter the Identify verification by card details and click Next

This will then take us to a section where we need to verify that we are who we are by providing some credit card information.

All we need to do here is provide a valid credit card, and the associated details.

To do this we just need to enter in all the credit card information and the billing address before clicking on the **Next** button.

dync
www.dynamicscompanions.com
Dynamics Companions

- 18 -

www.blindsquirrelpublishing.com
© 2019 Blind Squirrel Publishing, LLC , All Rights Reserved

BLIND SQUIRREL
PUBLISHING

Getting a Free Trial Azure Subscription

How to do it..

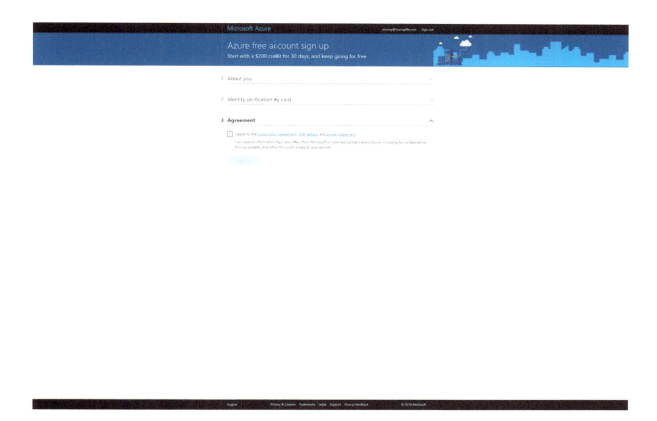

Step 7: Enter the Identify verification by card details and click Next

Finally, we will be taken to the last step, which is to confirm the agreement terms for the subscription.

www.dynamicscompanions.com
Dynamics Companions

- 19 -

www.blindsquirrelpublishing.com
© 2019 Blind Squirrel Publishing, LLC , All Rights Reserved

BLIND SQUIRREL
PUBLISHING

Getting a Free Trial Azure Subscription

How to do it..

Step 8: Change the I agree and click on the Sign up button

All we need to do here is confirm that we agree to the terms and conditions and sign on up.

To do this we will just need to change the **I agree** option and click on the **Sign up** button.

For this example, we will want to click on the **I agree** toggle switch and change it to the **Checked** value.

www.dynamicscompanions.com
Dynamics Companions

- 20 -

www.blindsquirrelpublishing.com
© 2019 Blind Squirrel Publishing, LLC , All Rights Reserved

BLIND SQUIRREL
PUBLISHING

Getting a Free Trial Azure Subscription

How to do it..

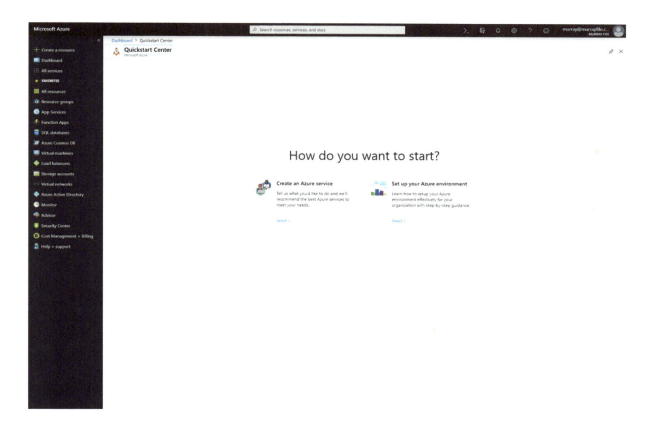

Step 8: Change the I agree and click on the Sign up button

After we have done that, we will be taken to the **QuickStart Center** and we will have a new subscription configured.

www.dynamicscompanions.com
Dynamics Companions

- 21 -

www.blindsquirrelpublishing.com
© 2019 Blind Squirrel Publishing, LLC , All Rights Reserved

BLIND SQUIRREL
PUBLISHING

Upgrading the Free Trial to a Pay-As-You-Go Subscription

Unfortunately, the free trial will not let us deploy out a demo instance because it is restricted to creating virtual machines that have only 4 cores, and the Cloud-hosted environment that we will want to deploy has 8 cored.

So, before we can continue, we will want to upgrade the subscription to a Pay-As-You-Go subscription. The good news is that since we signed up for the Free Trial subscription, we will still be able to take advantage of the first free month and the $200 in Azure credits that we were given on our account.

How to do it...

Step 1: Click on the Add button

Now we just need to upgrade our Free Trial subscription to a Pay-As-You-Go subscription. We will do this by adding a new subscription and then applying it to the Free Trial.

Click on the **Add** button.

Step 2: Click on the Pay-As-You-Go link

Since we have already used our free trial, we will not see that here anymore.

So, we will need to add a new subscription and select the **Pay-As-You-Go** option.

Click on the **Pay-As-You-Go** link.

Step 3: Click on the Upgrade link

Now we will be given the option to create a new subscription or upgrade the existing subscription to a Pay-As-You-Go subscription.

We will want to upgrade the Free Trial subscription to a Pay-As-You-Go subscription.

Click on the **Upgrade** link.

Step 4: Click on the Upgrade now button

This will open a dialog box asking us to upgrade the existing subscription.

We will use this to upgrade the Free Trial.

Click on the **Upgrade now** button.

Step 5: Click on the Close button

Then we will be asked for some upcharge options for the subscription which we can decline.

Click on the **Close** button.

Upgrading the Free Trial to a Pay-As-You-Go Subscription

How to do it...

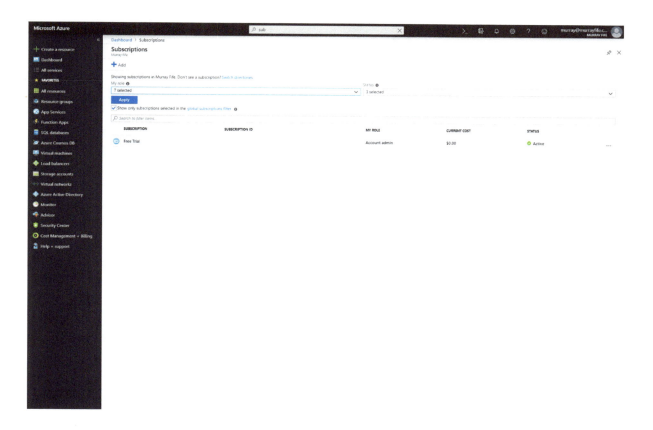

Step 1: Click on the Add button

Now we just need to upgrade our Free Trial subscription to a Pay-As-You-Go subscription. We will do this by adding a new subscription and then applying it to the Free Trial.

To do this just click on the **Add** button.

Upgrading the Free Trial to a Pay-As-You-Go Subscription

How to do it...

Step 2: Click on the Pay-As-You-Go link

Since we have already used our free trial, we will not see that here anymore.

So, we will need to add a new subscription and select the **Pay-As-You-Go** option.

To do this all we need to do is click on the **Pay-As-You-Go** link.

Upgrading the Free Trial to a Pay-As-You-Go Subscription

How to do it...

Step 3: Click on the Upgrade link

Now we will be given the option to create a new subscription or upgrade the existing subscription to a Pay-As-You-Go subscription.

We will want to upgrade the Free Trial subscription to a Pay-As-You-Go subscription.

To do this all we need to do is click on the **Upgrade** link.

www.dynamicscompanions.com
Dynamics Companions

- 25 -

www.blindsquirrelpublishing.com
© 2019 Blind Squirrel Publishing, LLC , All Rights Reserved

BLIND SQUIRREL
PUBLISHING

Upgrading the Free Trial to a Pay-As-You-Go Subscription

How to do it...

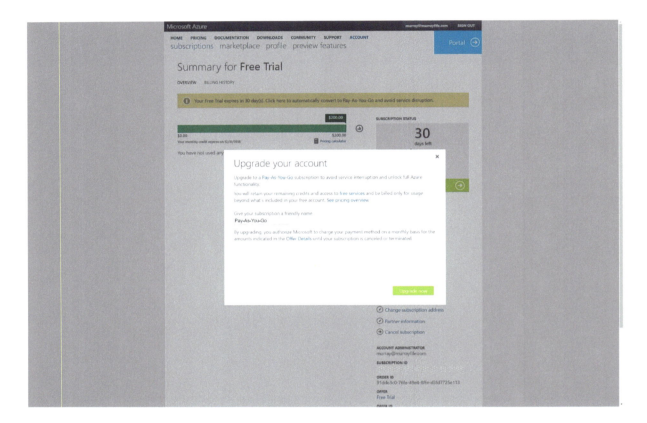

Step 4: Click on the Upgrade now button

This will open a dialog box asking us to upgrade the existing subscription.

We will use this to upgrade the Free Trial.

To do this all we need to do is click on the **Upgrade now** button.

Upgrading the Free Trial to a Pay-As-You-Go Subscripton

How to do it...

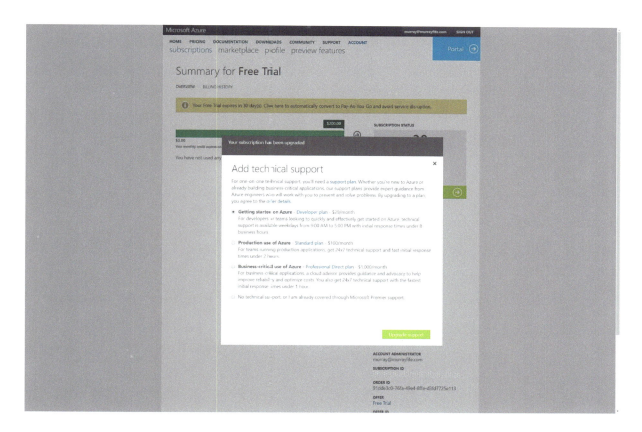

Step 5: Click on the Close button

Then we will be asked for some upcharge options for the subscription which we can decline.

To do this all we need to do is click on the **Close** button.

After we have done that we are done with the upgrade.

Adding the Dynamics Deployment Service as a Contributor

There is one last thing that we will want to do while we are still here in the subscription, and that is to add a service account called **Dynamics Deployment Service** to the subscription as a contributor.

This service is used by Lifecycle Services later in the setup to deploy out the Cloud-hosted environments. If this account is not linked to the subscription, then we will see a couple of problems with the deployment in the next steps.

How to do it...

Step 1: Select the Subscription

We will start off by selecting our subscription that we just created.

Select the subscription and open the details.

Step 2: Click on the Access control (AIM) button

Now we will want to open the **Access control** settings to see the users that have access to the subscription.

Click on the **Access control (AIM)** button.

Step 3: Click on the Add role assignment button

Now we will want to add a new role to the subscription.

Click on the **Add role assignment** button.

Step 4: Select the Role

Now we will want to mark the role as a **Contributor** to the subscription.

Click on the **Role** dropdown list and choose **Contributor**.

Step 5: Choose the Select

Now we will need to find the Dynamics Deployment Service from the list of users and services that are registered in Azure.

Click on the Select dropdown list and choose Dynamics Deployment Services [wsfed-enabled].

Step 6: Click on the Save button

Once the **Dynamics Deployment Service** is selected, we can save the selection and add the role to the subscription.

Click on the **Save** button.

Adding the Dynamics Deployment Service as a Contributor

How to do it...

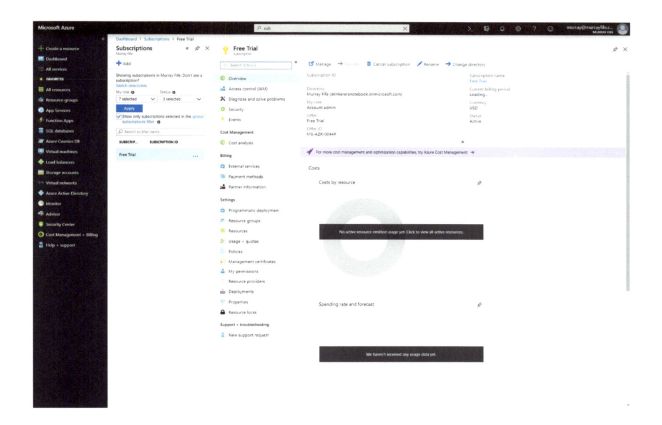

Step 1: Select the Subscription

We will start off by selecting our subscription that we just created.

To do this, just return to the subscriptions and select the subscription so that we can see the details.

www.dynamicscompanions.com
Dynamics Companions

- 29 -

www.blindsquirrelpublishing.com
© 2019 Blind Squirrel Publishing, LLC , All Rights Reserved

BLIND SQUIRREL
PUBLISHING

Adding the Dynamics Deployment Service as a Contributor

How to do it...

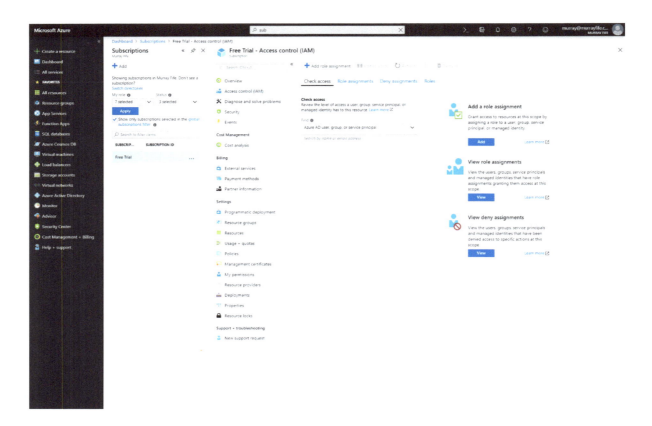

Step 2: Click on the Access control (AIM) button

Now we will want to open the **Access control** settings to see the users that have access to the subscription.

To do this all we need to do is click on the **Access control (AIM)** button.

www.dynamicscompanions.com
Dynamics Companions

- 30 -

www.blindsquirrelpublishing.com
© 2019 Blind Squirrel Publishing, LLC , All Rights Reserved

BLIND SQUIRREL
PUBLISHING

Adding the Dynam cs Deployment Service as a Contributor

How to do it...

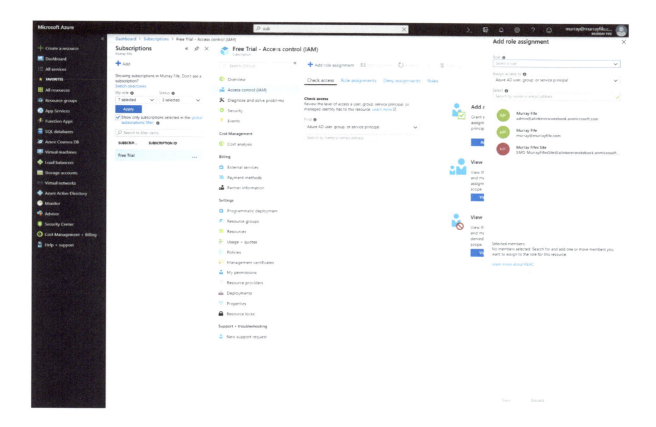

Step 3: Click on the Add role assignment button

Now we will want to add a new role to the subscription.

To do this just click on the **Add role assignment** button.

dync
www.dynamicscompanions.com
Dynamics Companions

- 31 -

www.blindsquirrelpublishing.com
© 2019 Blind Squirrel Publishing, LLC , All Rights Reserved

BLIND SQUIRREL
PUBLISHING

Adding the Dynamics Deployment Service as a Contributor

How to do it...

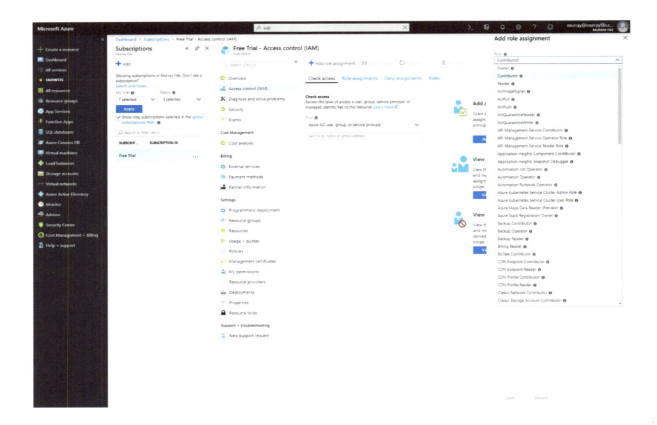

Step 4: Select the Role

Now we will want to mark the role as a **Contributor** to the subscription.

To do this just pick the **Role** value from the dropdown list.

This time, we will want to click on the **Role** dropdown list and pick **Contributor**.

www.dynamicscompanions.com
Dynamics Companions

- 32 -

www.blindsquirrelpublishing.com
© 2019 Blind Squirrel Publishing, LLC , All Rights Reserved

BLIND SQUIRREL
PUBLISHING

Adding the Dynamics Deployment Service as a Contributor

How to do it...

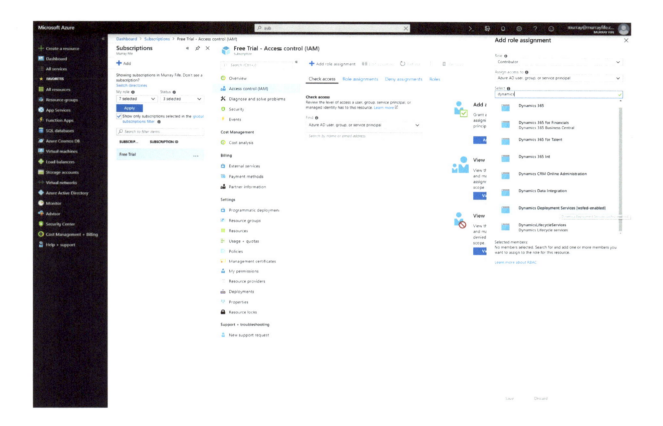

Step 5: Choose the Select

Now we will need to find the Dynamics Deployment Service from the list of users and services that are registered in Azure.

To do this just select the **Select** option from the dropdown list.

For this example, we will want to click on the **Select** dropdown list and select **Dynamics Deployment Services [wsfed-enabled]**.

www.dynamicscompanions.com
Dynamics Companions

- 33 -

www.blindsquirrelpublishing.com
© 2019 Blind Squirrel Publishing, LLC , All Rights Reserved

BLIND SQUIRREL
PUBLISHING

Adding the Dynamics Deployment Service as a Contributor

How to do it...

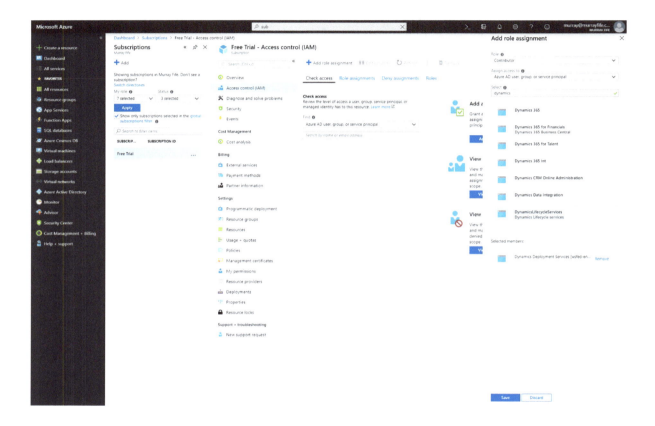

Step 6: Click on the Save button

Once the **Dynamics Deployment Service** is selected, we can save the selection and add the role to the subscription.

To do this just click on the **Save** button.

www.dynamicscompanions.com
Dynamics Companions

- 34 -

www.blindsquirrelpublishing.com
© 2019 Blind Squirrel Publishing, LLC , All Rights Reserved

BLIND SQUIRREL
PUBLISHING

Adding the Dynamics Deployment Service as a Contributor

How to do it...

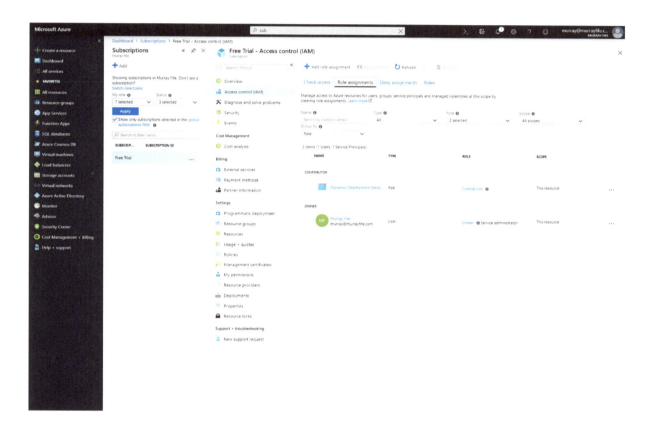

Step 6: Click on the Save button

After we have done that we are done with the setup of the subscription and the security roles.

dync
www.dynamicscompanions.com
Dynamics Companions

- 35 -

www.blindsquirrelpublishing.com
© 2019 Blind Squirrel Publishing, LLC , All Rights Reserved

BLIND SQUIRREL PUBLISHING

Review

The first step in the setup of the Cloud-hosted environment is done. We now have a subscription that we can use in Azure to pay for the environment.

Some other things that you may want to do if you like is set up a spending limit on the subscription, which will make sure that you don't get any surprise bills at the end of the month.

Creating a Cloud-hosted environment

Now that we have our subscription, we can move on to the creation of our Cloud Based Environment.

We will do this through the Lifecycle Services tool which is where we can link our Azure subscription to the environment, manage the environment, and access resources that we might need later to tweak Dynamics 365.

Topics Covered

- Creating a Lifecycle Services Project

- Configuring your Azure Subscription in Lifecycle Services

- Deploying a Cloud-hosted environment

- Opening Dynamics 365 for the f rst time

Creating a Lifecycle Services Project

We will start off by logging into Lifecycle Services and creating a project that we will use to manage all our Cloud-hosted Environments.

How to do it...

Step 1: Click on the + button

We will start off by logging into Lifecycle Services by going to http://Lifecycle Services.dynamics.com and then creating a new project.

Click on the **+** button.

Step 2: Update the Name

Let's start off by giving our project a name that we can reference it by.

Set the Name to Waterdeep Trading Company.

Step 3: Choose the Product name

Now we will select the version of Dynamics 365 that we want to create the project for.

Click on the Product name dropdown list and choose Microsoft Dynamics 365 for Finance and Operations.

Step 4: Select the Product version

Next, we will want to select the version that we want to create this project for.

Click on the Product version dropdown list and choose Microsoft Dynamics 365 for Finance and Operations.

Step 5: Choose the Industry and click on the Create button

Finally, we will want to select the Industry that we want to model this project against and then create the project.

Click on the **Industry** dropdown list and select **Distribution** and click on the **Create** button.

Creating a Lifecycle Services Project

How to do it...

Step 1: Click on the + button

We will start off by logging into Lifecycle Services by going to http://Lifecycle Services.dynamics.com and then creating a new project.

To do this all we need to do is click on the **+** button.

www.dynamicscompanions.com
Dynamics Companions

- 39 -

www.blindsquirrelpublishing.com
© 2019 Blind Squirrel Publishing, LLC , All Rights Reserved

BLIND SQUIRREL
PUBLISHING

Creating a Lifecycle Services Project

How to do it...

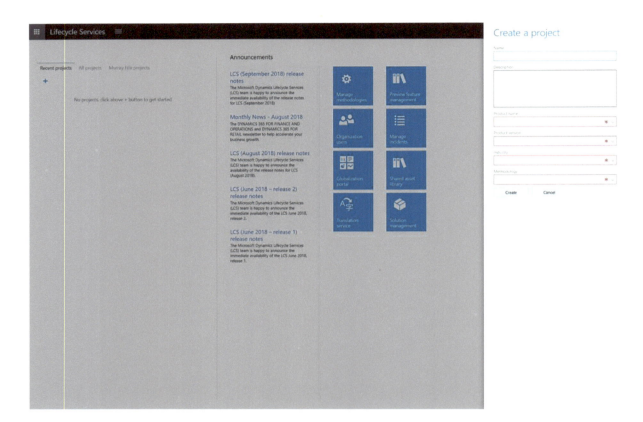

Step 1: Click on the + button

This will open the **Create a project** dialog box where we will be able to define the properties of the new Lifecycle Services (Lifecycle Services) project.

Creating a Lifecycle Services Project

How to do it...

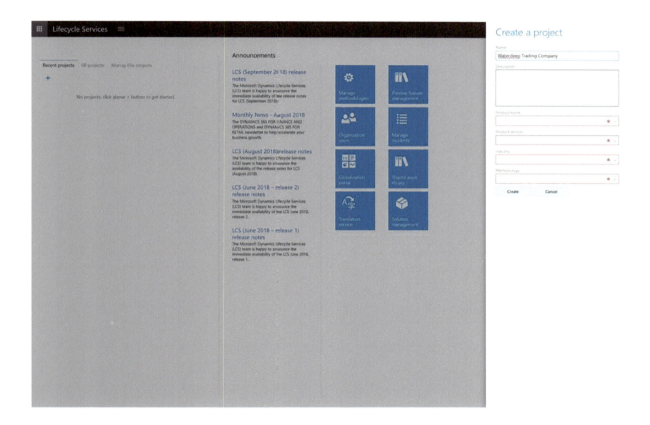

Step 2: Update the Name

Let's start off by giving our project a name that we can reference it by.

To do this we will just need to update the **Name** value.

For this example, we will want to set the **Name** to **Waterdeep Trading Company**.

Creating a Lifecycle Services Project

How to do it...

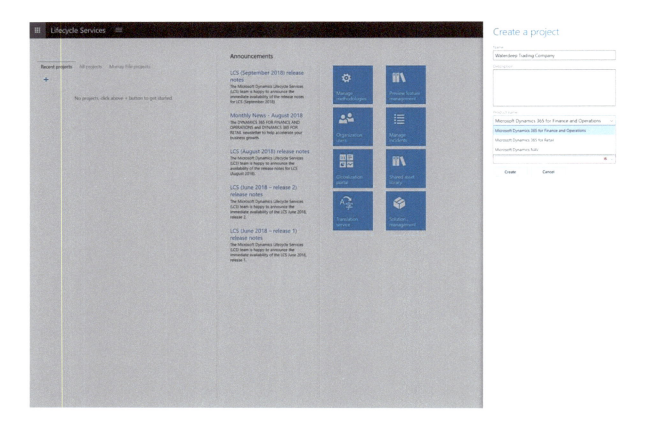

Step 3: Choose the Product name

Now we will select the version of Dynamics 365 that we want to create the project for.

To do this just select the **Product name** value from the dropdown list.

For this example, we will want to click on the **Product name** dropdown list and select **Microsoft Dynamics 365 for Finance and Operations**.

Creating a Lifecycle Services Project

How to do it...

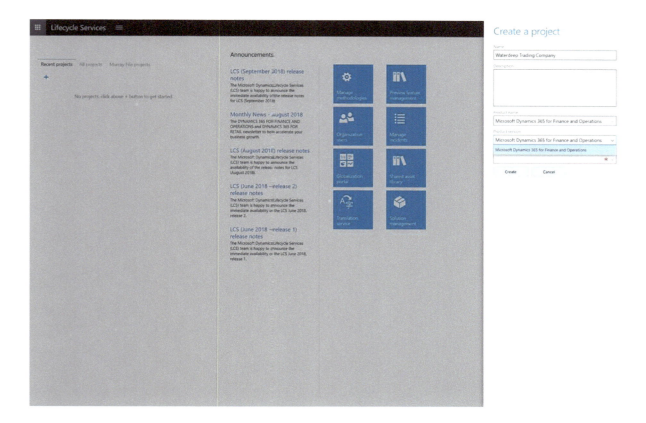

Step 4: Select the Product version

Next, we will want to select the version that we want to create this project for.

To do this just pick the **Product version** option from the dropdown list.

For this example, we will want to click on the **Product version** dropdown list and select **Microsoft Dynamics 365 for Finance and Operations**.

dync
dynamics companions

www.dynamicscompanions.com
Dynamics Companions

- 43 -

www.blindsquirrelpublishing.com
© 2019 Blind Squirrel Publishing, LLC , All Rights Reserved

BLIND SQUIRREL
PUBLISHING

Creating a Lifecycle Services Project

How to do it...

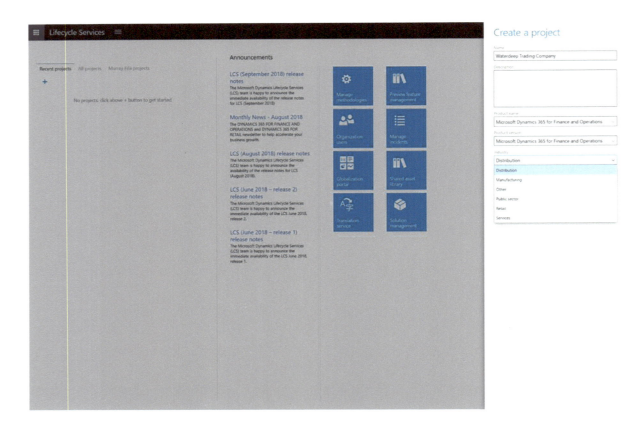

Step 5: Choose the Industry and click on the Create button

Finally, we will want to select the Industry that we want to model this project against and then create the project.

To do this we will just need to select the **Industry** value from the dropdown list and click on the **Create** button.

For this example, we will want to click on the **Industry** dropdown list and select **Distribution**.

Creating a Lifecycle Services Project

How to do it...

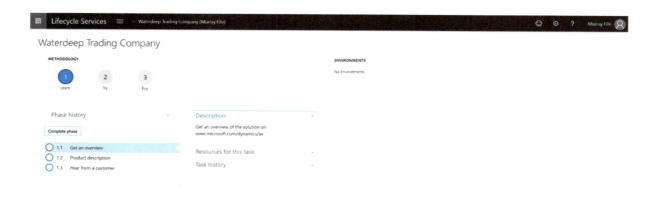

Step 5: Choose the Industry and click on the Create button

After a couple of seconds, we will be taken into the project that we just created.

dync
www.dynamicscompanions.com
Dynamics Companions

- 45 -

www.blindsquirrelpublishing.com
© 2019 Blind Squirrel Publishing, LLC, All Rights Reserved

BLIND SQUIRREL
PUBLISHING

Configuring your Azure Subscription in Lifecycle Services

Before we can create our Cloud-hosted environment though, there is one important step that we need to do and that is to link our Azure Subscription that we just signed up for to the Lifecycle Services project.

This will allow the deployment service to connect to Lifecycle Services and tell Lifecycle Services how we are going to pay for the service.

How to do it...

Step 1: Click on the Cloud-hosted environments button

We will do this by opening the **Cloud-hosted environments** management page from within our Lifecycle Services project.

Click on the Cloud-hosted environments button.

Step 2: Click on the Yes button

When the page is displayed, we will get a notice that is telling us that we do not have an Azure connector (i.e. a Subscription) linked to our project.

Before we continue, we will want to set this up.

Click on the **Yes** button.

Step 3: Click on the Authorize link

That will take us to the **Azure connectors** settings area within the **Project settings** where we will be able to link the azure subscription to the project.

There are two steps in this process, the first is to authorize the Dynamics Deployment Service

to connect to the project and then the creation of the connector.

We will start by authorizing the service to communicate with Lifecycle Services.

Click on the **Authorize** link.

Step 4: Click on the Authorize link

This will take us to a page where we can allow the **Dynamics Deployment Service** to connect to Lifecycle Services.

All we need to do here is Authorize the connection.

Click on the **Authorize** link.

Step 5: Click on the Account button

We will then need to authorize the connection by selecting the account that we will be using for the project.

Click on the **Account** button.

Step 6: Click on the Accept button

Then we will see all the different services that the Deployment Service will be given access to within the organization.

We will need to accept all of these before we can continue.

Click on the **Accept** button.

Step 7: Click on the Add button

Now we can perform the second step of the setup of the **Azure connector** which is to link our Azure subscription to the project within the **Azure connectors** section of the **Project settings**.

We will want to add a new connector now.

Click on the **Add** button.

Step 8: Update the Name

We will start off by naming the Connector that we are adding to the project.

Set the Name to Azure Subscription.

Step 9: Update the Azure subscription ID

Next, we will want to tell the project the Azure Subscription that we will be connecting to the project.

Type in the Azure subscription ID

Step 10: Change the Configure to use Azure Resource Manager (ARM) and click on the Next button

Before we finish this step, we will want to turn on the option for Azure Resource Manager to connect to the tenant. This will allow it to complete the deployment for us and then we can move on.

Toggle the **Configure to use Azure Resource Manager (ARM)** switch and set it to **Yes** and click on the **Next** button.

Step 11: Click on the Next button

Next, we will be taken to a step where Lifecycle Services will check that all the setup for the subscription is correct.

If no services are shown, then we may need to prod Lifecycle Services a little before we move to the next step.

Click on the **Next** button.

Step 12: Click on the Next button

We should now see the **Dynamics Deployment Service** is discovered as a **Contributor** in the subscription, and that it is valid.

That will allow us to move on to the next step in the setup.

Click on the **Next** button.

Step 13: Click on the Download button

Now we need to set up the security to connect the Azure Subscription with our Lifecycle Services project. We do this by adding a security certificate that Lifecycle Services provides us with the Azure Subscription.

We will start off this step by downloading the Security Certificate.

Click on the **Download** button.

That will download a certificate for us that we can then save away for the next step in the configuration.

Step 14: Click on the Management certificates link

Now we will want to return to the Azure Portal and select the Azure subscription that we created earlier on and go to the area where all the security certificates are managed.

Click on the Management certificates link.

Step 15: Click on the Upload button

From here we will be able to upload the certificate that we just downloaded from Lifecycle Services.

Click on the **Upload** button.

Step 16: Click on the Select a file button

This will open the **Upload Certificates** dialog.

From here we will be able to upload the certificate that we just got from Lifecycle Services.

Click on the **Select a file** button.

Step 17: Click on the LifecycleServicesDeploloyment.cer button and click on the Open button

When the File explorer is displayed, we will want to select the **LifecycleServicesDeploloyment.cer** file.

Click on the **LifecycleServicesDeploloyment.cer** button and click on the **Open** button.

Step 18: Click on the Upload button

Now we can upload the certificate to the Azure subscription.

Click on the **Upload** button.

Step 19: Click on the Next button

Now we can return to Lifecycle Services and resume the setup of the Azure connector.

Click on the **Next** button.

Next, we will be asked for the region that we want to deploy the services connected to this subscription.

Step 20: Select the Azure region

Here we can select any of the available Azure regions from the dropdown list. We will choose one that is geographically close to us, but you can choose any one that you like.

Click on the **Azure region** dropdown list and choose **East US**.

Step 21: Click on the Connect button

Now we can connect the Azure subscription to our Lifecycle Services project.

Click on the **Connect** button.

Configuring your Azure Subscription in Lifecycle Services

How to do it...

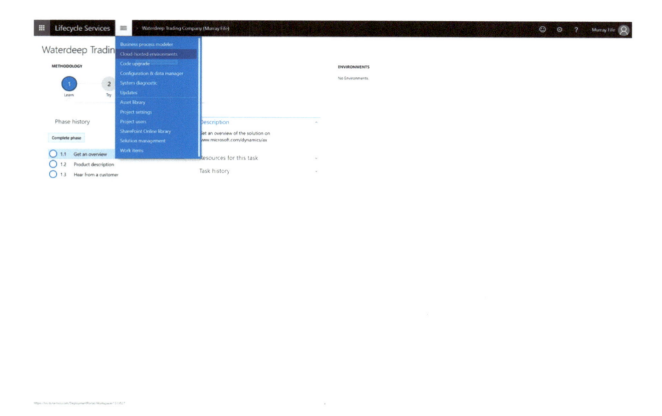

Step 1: Click on the Cloud-hosted environments button

We will do this by opening the **Cloud-hosted environments** management page from within our Lifecycle Services project.

To do this all we need to do is click on the **Cloud-hosted environments** button.

www.dynamicscompanions.com
Dynamics Companions

- 49 -

www.blindsquirrelpublishing.com
© 2019 Blind Squirrel Publishing, LLC , All Rights Reserved

BLIND SQUIRREL
PUBLISHING

Configuring your Azure Subscription in Lifecycle Services

How to do it...

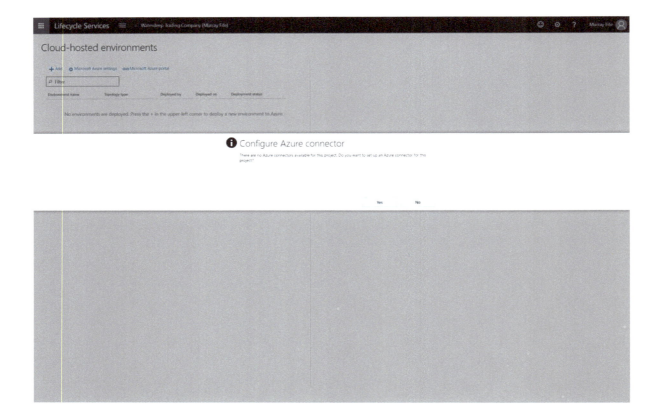

Step 2: Click on the Yes button

When the page is displayed, we will get a notice that is telling us that we do not have an Azure connector (i.e. a Subscription) linked to our project.

Before we continue, we will want to set this up.

To do this just click on the **Yes** button.

Configuring your Azure Subscription in Lifecycle Services

How to do it...

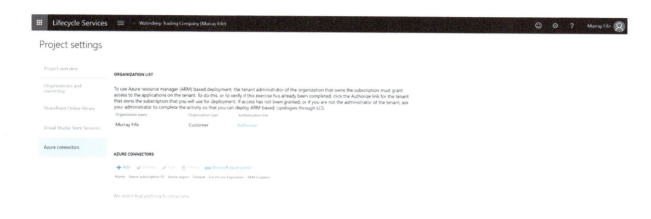

Step 3: Click on the Authorize link

That will take us to the **Azure connectors** settings area within the **Project settings** where we will be able to link the azure subscription to the project.

There are two steps in this process, the first is to authorize the Dynamics Deployment Service to connect to the project and then the creation of the connector.

We will start by authorizing the service to communicate with Lifecycle Services.

To do this all we need to do is click on the **Authorize** link.

www.dynamicscompanions.com
Dynamics Companions

- 51 -

www.blindsquirrelpublishing.com
© 2019 Blind Squirrel Publishing, LLC , All Rights Reserved

BLIND SQUIRREL
PUBLISHING

Configuring your Azure Subscription in Lifecycle Services

How to do it...

Step 4: Click on the Authorize link

This will take us to a page where we can allow the **Dynamics Deployment Service** to connect to Lifecycle Services.

All we need to do here is Authorize the connection.

To do this all we need to do is click on the **Authorize** link.

www.dynamicscompanions.com
Dynamics Companions

- 52 -

www.blindsquirrelpublishing.com
© 2019 Blind Squirrel Publishing, LLC , All Rights Reserved

BLIND SQUIRREL
PUBLISHING

Configuring your Azure Subscription in Lifecycle Services

How to do it...

Step 5: Click on the Account button

We will then need to authorize the connect on by selecting the account that we will be using for the project.

To do this just click on the **Account** button.

dync
www.dynamicscompanions.com
Dynamics Companions

- 53 -

www.blindsquirrelpublishing.com
© 2019 Blind Squirrel Publishing, LLC , All Rights Reserved

BLIND SQUIRREL
PUBLISHING

Configuring your Azure Subscription in Lifecycle Services

How to do it...

Step 6: Click on the Accept button

Then we will see all the different services that the Deployment Service will be given access to within the organization.

We will need to accept all of these before we can continue.

To do this just click on the **Accept** button.

Configuring your Azure Subscription in Lifecycle Services

How to do it...

Step 6: Click on the Accept button

After we have done that, we will be returned to the **Grant admin consent** page and we can continue.

www.dynamicscompanions.com
Dynamics Companions

- 55 -

www.blindsquirrelpublishing.com
© 2019 Blind Squirrel Publishing, LLC , All Rights Reserved

BLIND SQUIRREL
PUBLISHING

Configuring your Azure Subscription in Lifecycle Services

How to do it...

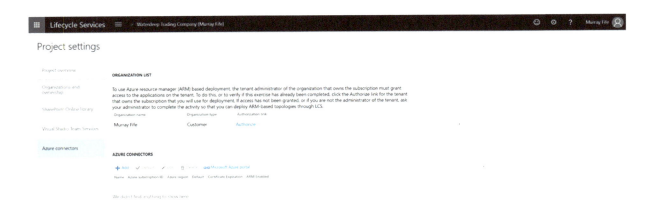

Step 7: Click on the Add button

Now we can perform the second step of the setup of the **Azure connector** which is to link our Azure subscription to the project within the **Azure connectors** section of the **Project settings**.

We will want to add a new connector now.

To do this all we need to do is click on the **Add** button.

Configuring your Azure Subscription in Lifecycle Services

How to do it...

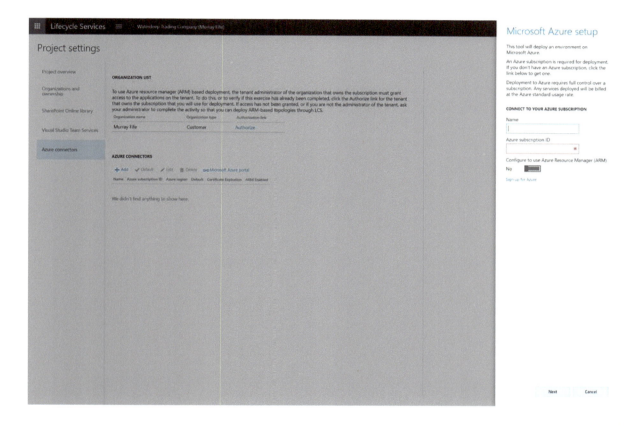

Step 7: Click on the Add button

This will open the **Microsoft Azure setup** dialog box where we will be able to give it all the information about our Subscription.

dync
www.dynamicscompanions.com
Dynamics Companions

- 57 -

www.blindsquirrelpublishing.com
© 2019 Blind Squirrel Publishing, LLC , All Rights Reserved

BLIND SQUIRREL
PUBLISHING

Configuring your Azure Subscription in Lifecycle Services

How to do it...

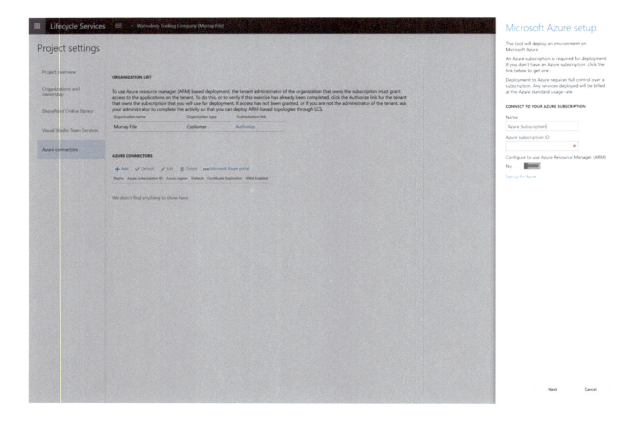

Step 8: Update the Name

We will start off by naming the Connector that we are adding to the project.

To do this just change the **Name** value.

For this example, we will want to set the **Name** to **Azure Subscription**.

Configuring your Azure Subscription in Lifecycle Services

How to do it...

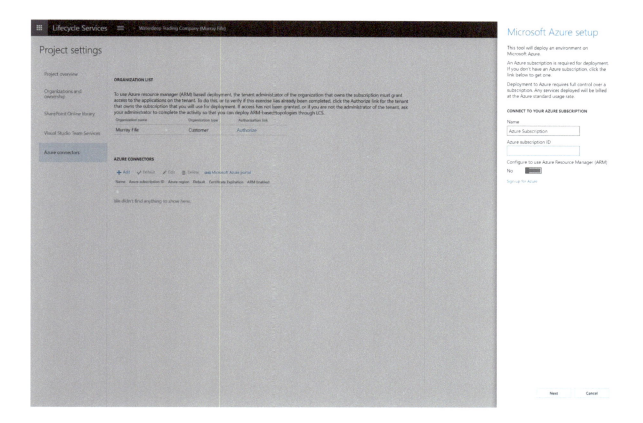

Step 9: Update the Azure subscription ID

Next, we will want to tell the project the Azure Subscription that we will be connecting to the project.

To do this we will just need to update the **Azure subscription ID** value.

This time, we will want to type in the **Azure subscription ID**

dync
www.dynamicscompanions.com
Dynamics Companions

- 59 -

www.blindsquirrelpublishing.com
© 2019 Blind Squirrel Publishing, LLC , All Rights Reserved

BLIND SQUIRREL
PUBLISHING

Configuring your Azure Subscription in Lifecycle Services

How to do it...

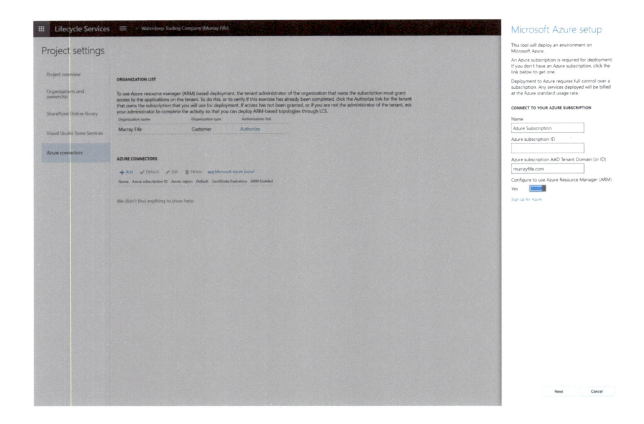

Step 10: Change the Configure to use Azure Resource Manager (ARM) and click on the Next button

Before we finish this step, we will want to turn on the option for Azure Resource Manager to connect to the tenant. This will allow it to complete the deployment for us and then we can move on.

Make sure that the **Azure subscription AAD Tenant Domain (or ID)** field is set top the domain where you are hosting the subscription. If this is different (i.e. you are using someone else's subscription, then you will want to change this Tenant ID.

To do this just switch the **Configure to use Azure Resource Manager (ARM)** value and click on the **Next** button.

For this example, we will want to click on the **Configure to use Azure Resource Manager (ARM)** toggle switch and update it to the **Yes** value.

Configuring your Azure Subscription in Lifecycle Services

How to do it...

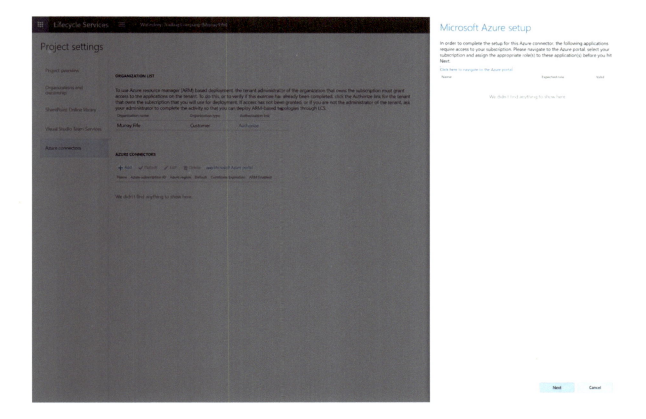

Step 11: Click on the Next button

Next, we will be taken to a step where Lifecycle Services will check that all the setup for the subscription is correct.

If no services are shown, then we may need to prod Lifecycle Services a little before we move to the next step.

To do this just click on the **Next** button.

www.dynamicscompanions.com
Dynamics Companions

- 61 -

www.blindsquirrelpublishing.com
© 2019 Blind Squirrel Publishing, LLC , All Rights Reserved

BLIND SQUIRREL
PUBLISHING

Configuring your Azure Subscription in Lifecycle Services

How to do it...

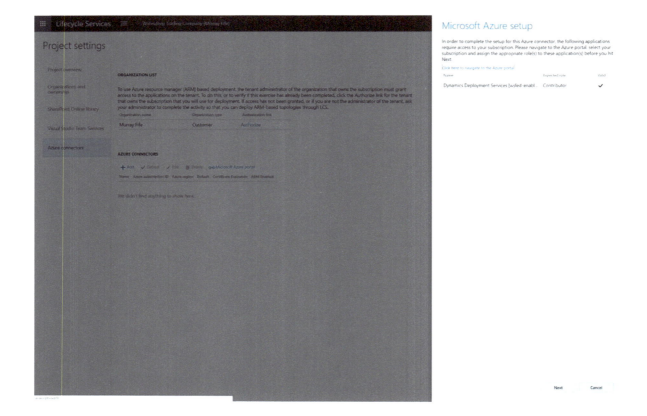

Step 12: Click on the Next button

We should now see the **Dynamics Deployment Service** is discovered as a **Contributor** in the subscription, and that it is valid.

That will allow us to move on to the next step in the setup.

To do this just click on the **Next** button.

www.dynamicscompanions.com
Dynamics Companions

- 62 -

www.blindsquirrelpublishing.com
© 2019 Blind Squirrel Publishing, LLC , All Rights Reserved

BLIND SQUIRREL
PUBLISHING

Configuring your Azure Subscription in Lifecycle Services

How to do it...

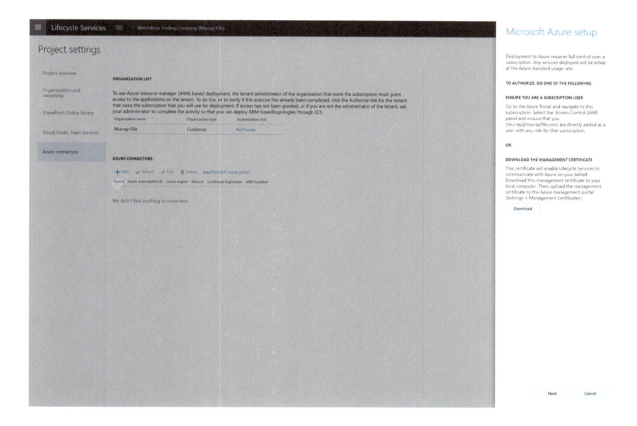

Step 13: Click on the Download button

Now we need to set up the security to connect the Azure Subscription with our Lifecycle Services project. We do this by adding a security certificate that Lifecycle Services provides us with the Azure Subscription.

We will start off this step by downloading the Security Certificate.

To do this all we need to do is click on the **Download** button.

www.dynamicscompanions.com
Dynamics Companions

- 63 -

www.blindsquirrelpublishing.com
© 2019 Blind Squirrel Publishing, LLC , All Rights Reserved

BLIND SQUIRREL
PUBLISHING

Configuring your Azure Subscription in Lifecycle Services

How to do it...

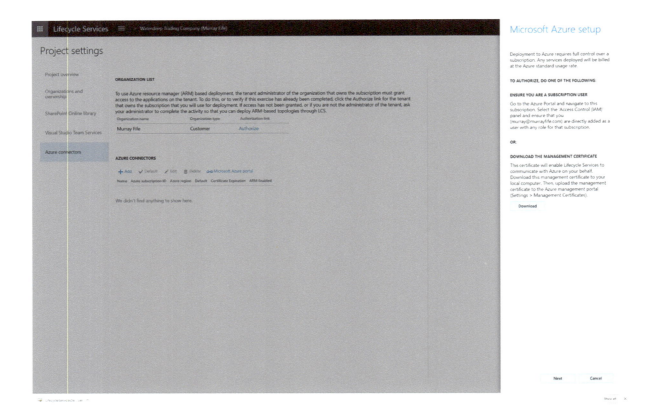

Step 13: Click on the Download button

That will download a certificate for us that we can then save away for the next step in the configuration.

www.dynamicscompanions.com
Dynamics Companions

- 64 -

www.blindsquirrelpublishing.com
© 2019 Blind Squirrel Publishing, LLC , All Rights Reserved

BLIND SQUIRREL
PUBLISHING

Configuring your Azure Subscription in Lifecycle Services

How to do it...

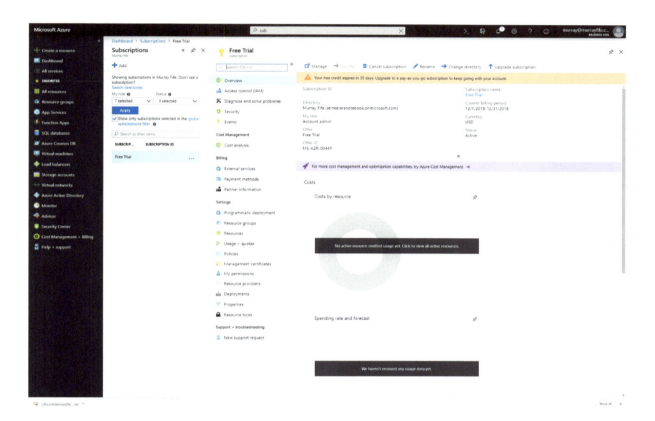

Step 14: Click on the Management certificates link

Now we will want to return to the Azure Portal and select the Azure subscription that we created earlier on and go to the area where all the security certificates are managed.

To do this all we need to do is click on the **Management certificates** link.

www.dynamicscompanions.com
Dynamics Companions

- 65 -

www.blindsquirrelpublishing.com
© 2019 Blind Squirrel Publishing, LLC , All Rights Reserved

BLIND SQUIRREL
PUBLISHING

Configuring your Azure Subscription in Lifecycle Services

How to do it...

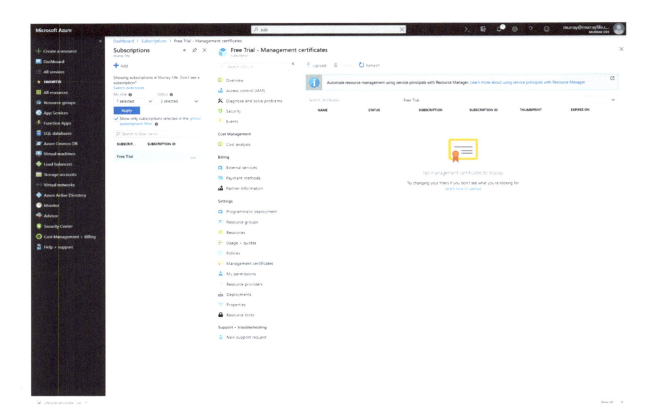

Step 15: Click on the Upload button

From here we will be able to upload the certificate that we just downloaded from Lifecycle Services.

To do this all we need to do is click on the **Upload** button.

www.dynamicscompanions.com
Dynamics Companions

- 66 -

www.blindsquirrelpublishing.com
© 2019 Blind Squirrel Publishing, LLC , All Rights Reserved

BLIND SQUIRREL
PUBLISHING

Configuring your Azure Subscription in Lifecycle Services

How to do it...

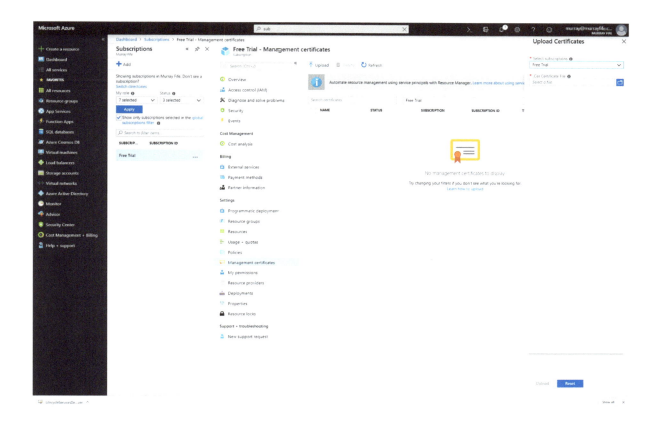

Step 16: Click on the Select a file button

This will open the **Upload Certificates** dialog.

From here we will be able to upload the certificate that we just got from Lifecycle Services.

To do this just click on the **Select a file** button.

www.dynamicscompanions.com
Dynamics Companions

- 67 -

www.blindsquirrelpublishing.com
© 2019 Blind Squirrel Publishing, LLC , All Rights Reserved

BLIND SQUIRREL
PUBLISHING

Configuring your Azure Subscription in Lifecycle Services

How to do it...

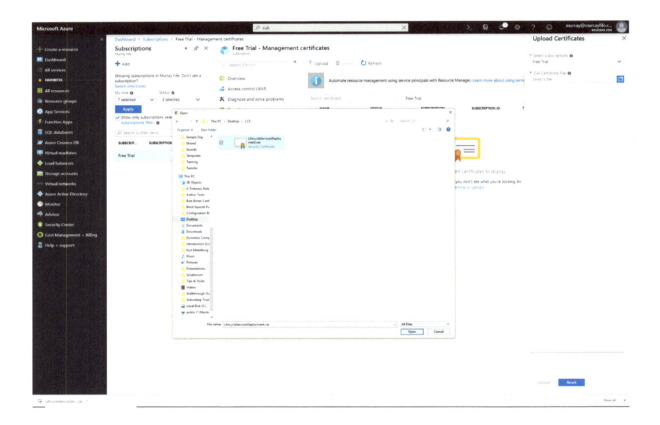

Step 17: Click on the LifecycleServicesDeploloyment.cer button and click on the Open button

When the File explorer is displayed, we will want to select the **LifecycleServicesDeploloyment.cer** file.

To do this all we need to do is click on the **LifecycleServicesDeploloyment.cer** button and click on the **Open** button.

Configuring your Azure Subscription in Lifecycle Services

How to do it...

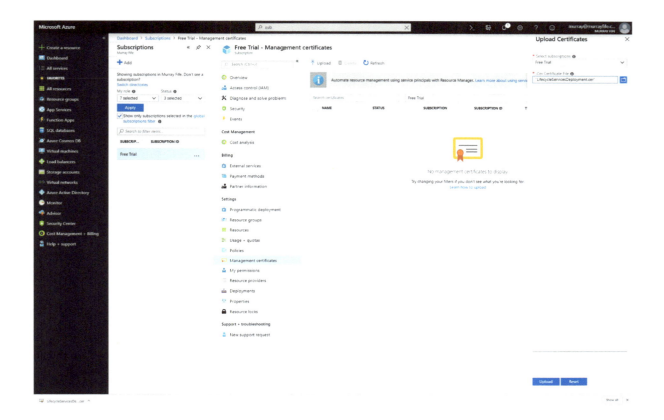

Step 18: Click on the Upload button

Now we can upload the certificate to the Azure subscription.

To do this just click on the **Upload** button.

dync
www.dynamicscompanions.com
Dynamics Companions

- 69 -

www.blindsquirrelpublishing.com
© 2019 Blind Squirrel Publishing, LLC , All Rights Reserved

BLIND SQUIRREL
PUBLISHING

Configuring your Azure Subscription in Lifecycle Services

How to do it...

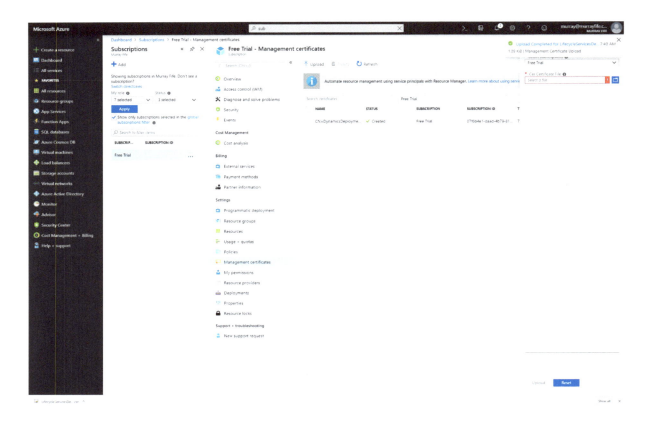

Step 18: Click on the Upload button

After we have done that, we will see that the certificate is associated with the subscription and we can continue.

Configuring your Azure Subscription in Lifecycle Services

How to do it...

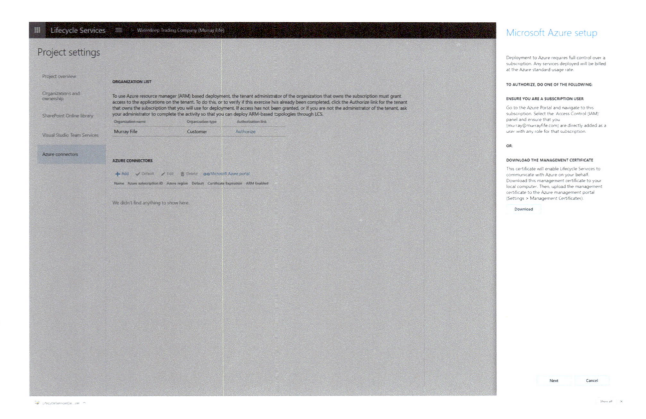

Step 19: Click on the Next button

Now we can return to Lifecycle Services and resume the setup of the Azure connector.

To do this all we need to do is click on the **Next** button.

dync
www.dynamicscompanions.com
Dynamics Companions

- 71 -

www.blindsquirrelpublishing.com
© 2019 Blind Squirrel Publishing, LLC , All Rights Reserved

BLIND SQUIRREL
PUBLISHING

Configuring your Azure Subscription in Lifecycle Services

How to do it...

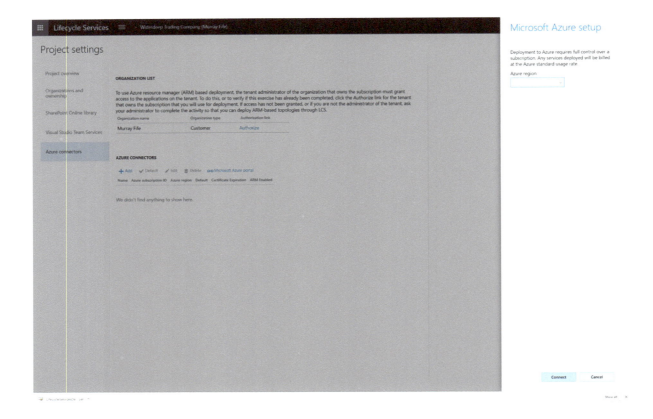

Step 19: Click on the Next button

Next, we will be asked for the region that we want to deploy the services connected to this subscription.

Configuring your Azure Subscription in Lifecycle Services

How to do it...

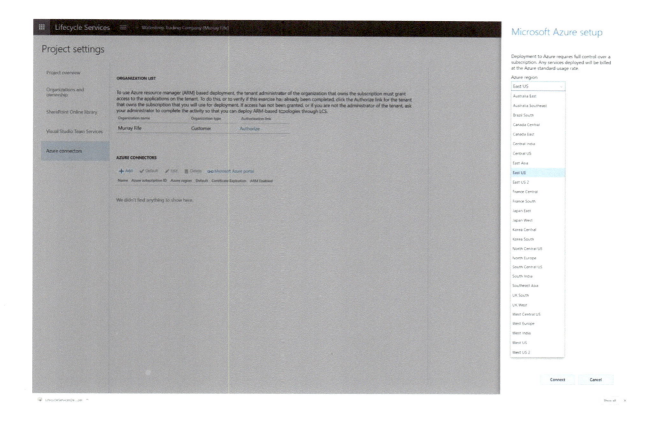

Step 20: Select the Azure region

Here we can select any of the available Azure regions from the dropdown list. We will choose one that is geographically close to us, but you can choose any one that you like.

To do this just select the **Azure region** value from the dropdown list.

For this example, we will want to click on the **Azure region** dropdown list and pick **East US**.

www.dynamicscompanions.com
Dynamics Companions

- 73 -

www.blindsquirrelpublishing.com
© 2019 Blind Squirrel Publishing, LLC , All Rights Reserved

BLIND SQUIRREL
PUBLISHING

Configuring your Azure Subscription in Lifecycle Services

How to do it...

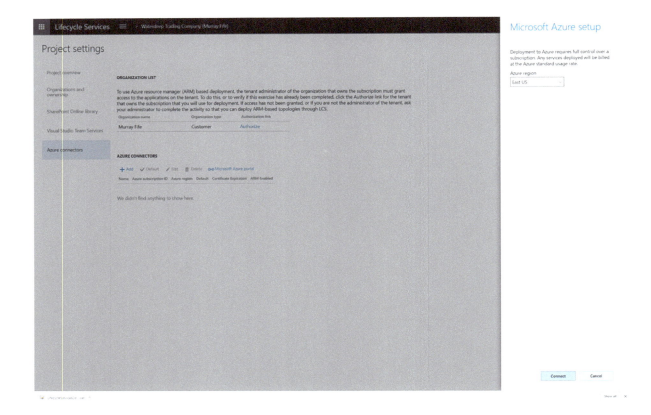

Step 21: Click on the Connect button

Now we can connect the Azure subscription to our Lifecycle Services project.

To do this all we need to do is click on the **Connect** button.

www.dynamicscompanions.com
Dynamics Companions

- 74 -

www.blindsquirrelpublishing.com
© 2019 Blind Squirrel Publishing, LLC , All Rights Reserved

BLIND SQUIRREL
PUBLISHING

Configuring your Azure Subscription in Lifecycle Services

How to do it...

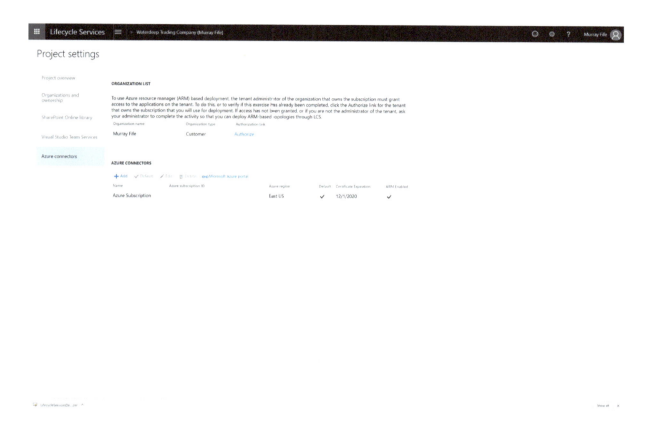

Step 21: Click on the Connect button

When we return to the **Azure connectors** page, we will see that we now have an Azure connector that we can use to deploy our Cloud-hosted environment with.

dync
www.dynamicscompanions.com
Dynamics Companions

- 75 -

www.blindsquirrelpublishing.com
© 2019 Blind Squirrel Publishing, LLC , All Rights Reserved

BLIND SQUIRREL
PUBLISHING

Deploying a Cloud-hosted environment

We have now set up all the subscriptions and the Azure connections within Lifecycle Services, we can move onto the last step in the process, which is the creation of our first Cloud-hosted environment for Dynamics 365.

How to do it...

Step 1: Click on the Cloud-hosted environments button

To do this we will want to switch to the Cloud-hosted environments section within Lifecycle Services.

Click on the **Cloud-hosted environments** button from within the Lifecycle Services hamburger menu.

Step 2: Click on the Add button

This will take us to the **Cloud-hosted environments** page where we can manage all the environments we will use for this project.

All we need to do is create a new environment.

Click on the **Add** button.

Step 3: Click on the Next button

This will open the wizard dialog that will step us through the setup of the Cloud-hosted environment.

The first step is to select the Application version and the Platform version that we want to deploy. By default, we will see the latest versions, and unless you want to go retro, we will keep these defaults and continue.

Click on the **Next** button.

Step 4: Click on the DEMO button

Next, we will want to select the type of environment that we want to create.

Click on the **DEMO** button.

That will take us to the final step in the deployment process which is to name the environment and confirm the deployment of the environment.

Step 5: Update the Environment name

Let's start off by giving our environment a name.

Set the Environment name to WDTC.

Step 6: Update the By selecting the checkbox... and click on the Next button

And then we will want to accept that we will pay for all the charges that are incurred by this environment and continuing.

Set the By selecting the checkbox... to Checked and click on the Next button.

Step 7: Click on the Deploy button

We will be given one last chance to confirm that we want to deploy the Cloud-hosted environment which we will want to accept.

Click on the **Deploy** button.

This will start off the process of deploying out the cloud hosted environment for us. All we need to do now is to wait for the Cloud-hosted environment to be deployed.

Step 8: Click on the Environment button

After a few hours, check back on the Cloud-hosted environment and you will see that the Deployment status will eventually change to a **Deployed** status which means that it is available for us to use.

We can see more information about the Cloud-hosted environment by clicking on the environment.

Click on the **Environment** button.

Step 9: Click on the Full details button

This will give us a summary of the Cloud-housed environment with all the access details and links to log into Dynamics 365.

We can see more information about the environment by accessing the full details of the deployment.

Click on the **Full details** button.

Step 10: Change the Pin this environment to the Dynamics 365 home page

From here we can make a small change which is to add the tile for Dynamics 365 to the home page for Dynamics 365. This is useful because it gives us an easy way to open Dynamics 365.

Toggle the Pin this environment to the Dynamics 365 home page switch And set it to Yes.

Step 11: Click on the Log on to environment button

Alternatively, we can log on to Dynamics 365 by selecting the Login button in the top right of the page and selecting the way that we want to access the cloud-hosted environment.

Click on the **Log on to environment** button.

Deploying a Cloud-hosted environment

How to do it...

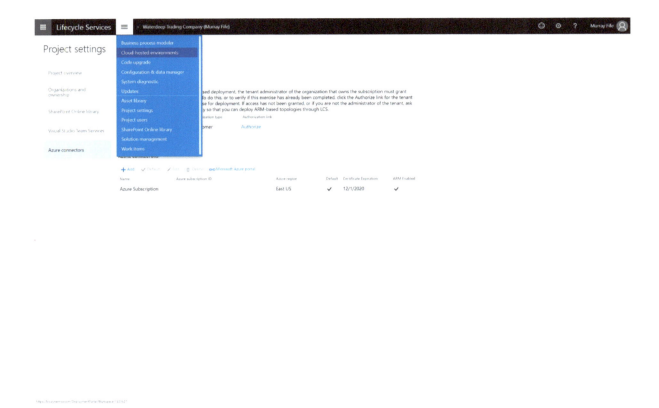

Step 1: Click on the Cloud-hosted environments button

To do this we will want to switch to the Cloud-hosted environments section within Lifecycle Services.

To do this just click on the **Cloud-hosted environments** button from within the Lifecycle Services hamburger menu.

Deploying a Cloud-hosted environment

How to do it...

Step 2: Click on the Add button

This will take us to the **Cloud-hosted environments** page where we can manage all the environments we will use for this project.

All we need to do is create a new environment.

To do this just click on the **Add** button.

www.dynamicscompanions.com
Dynamics Companions

- 79 -

www.blindsquirrelpublishing.com
© 2019 Blind Squirrel Publishing, LLC , All Rights Reserved

BLIND SQUIRREL
PUBLISHING

Deploying a Cloud-hosted environment

How to do it...

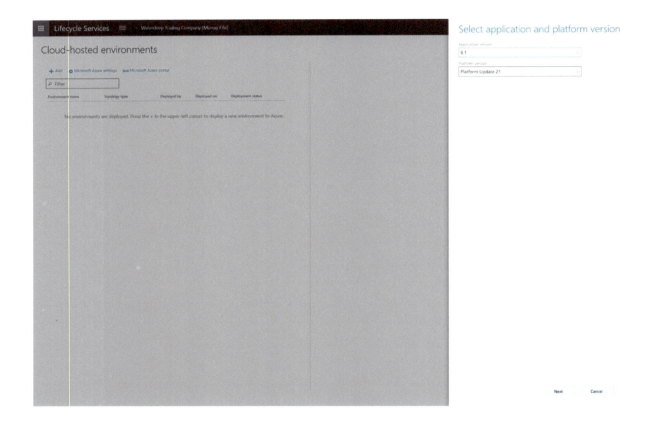

Step 3: Click on the Next button

This will open the wizard dialog that will step us through the setup of the Cloud-hosted environment.

The first step is to select the Application version and the Platform version that we want to deploy. By default, we will see the latest versions, and unless you want to go retro, we will keep these defaults and continue.

To do this all we need to do is click on the **Next** button.

Deploying a Cloud-hosted environment

How to do it...

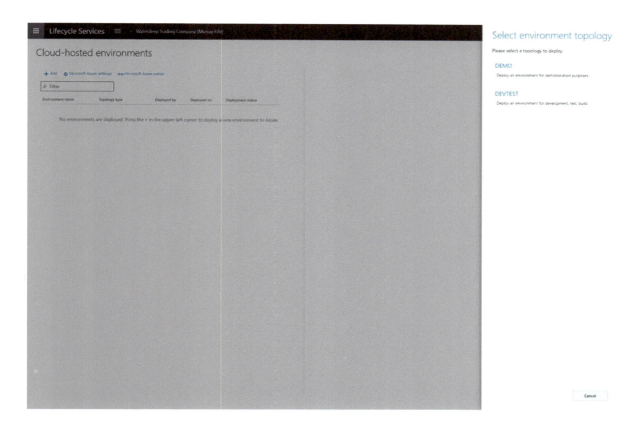

Step 4: Click on the DEMO button

Next, we will want to select the type of environment that we want to create.

To do this just click on the **DEMO** button.

www.dynamicscompanions.com
Dynamics Companions

- 81 -

www.blindsquirrelpublishing.com
© 2019 Blind Squirrel Publishing, LLC , All Rights Reserved

BLIND SQUIRREL
PUBLISHING

Deploying a Cloud-hosted environment

How to do it...

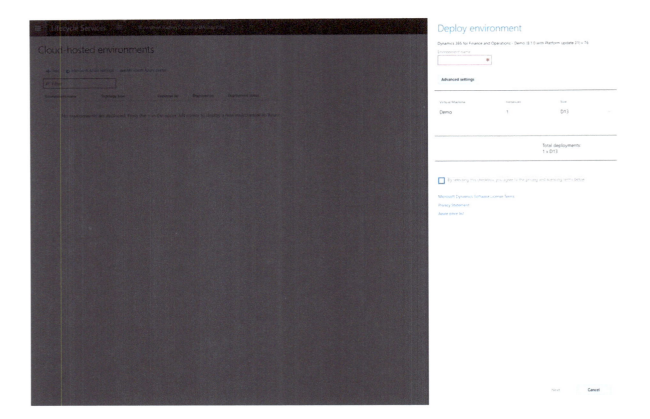

Step 4: Click on the DEMO button

That will take us to the final step in the deployment process which is to name the environment and confirm the deployment of the environment.

www.dynamicscompanions.com
Dynamics Companions

- 82 -

www.blindsquirrelpublishing.com
© 2019 Blind Squirrel Publishing, LLC , All Rights Reserved

BLIND SQUIRREL
PUBLISHING

Deploying a Cloud-hosted environment

How to do it...

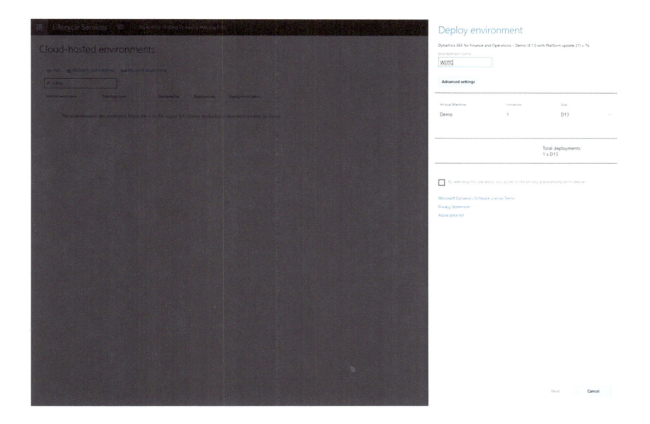

Step 5: Update the Environment name

Let's start off by giving our environment a name.

To do this we will just need to update the **Environment name** value.

For this example, we will want to set the **Environment name** to **WDTC**.

www.dynamicscompanions.com
Dynamics Companions

- 83 -

www.blindsquirrelpublishing.com
© 2019 Blind Squirrel Publishing, LLC , All Rights Reserved

BLIND SQUIRREL
PUBLISHING

Deploying a Cloud-hosted environment

How to do it...

Step 6: Update the By selecting the checkbox... and click on the Next button

And then we will want to accept that we will pay for all the charges that are incurred by this environment and continuing.

To do this just update the **By selecting the checkbox...** value and click on the **Next** button.

For this example, we will want to set the **By selecting the checkbox...** to **Checked**.

Deploying a Cloud-hosted environment

How to do it...

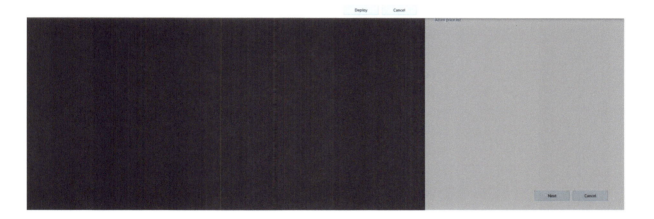

Step 7: Click on the Deploy button

We will be given one last chance to confirm that we want to deploy the Cloud-hosted environment which we will want to accept.

To do this all we need to do is click on the **Deploy** button.

www.dynamicscompanions.com
Dynamics Companions

- 85 -

www.blindsquirrelpublishing.com
© 2019 Blind Squirrel Publishing, LLC , All Rights Reserved

BLIND SQUIRREL
PUBLISHING

Deploying a Cloud-hosted environment

How to do it...

Step 7: Click on the Deploy button

This will start off the process of deploying out the cloud hosted environment for us. All we need to do now is to wait for the Cloud-hosted environment to be deployed.

Deploying a Cloud-hosted environment

How to do it...

Step 8: Click on the Environment button

After a few hours, check back on the Cloud-hosted environment and you will see that the Deployment status will eventually change to a **Deployed** status which means that it is available for us to use.

We can see more information about the Cloud-hosted environment by clicking on the environment.

To do this just click on the **Environment** button.

dync
Dynamics Companions

www.dynamicscompanions.com
Dynamics Companions

- 87 -

www.blindsquirrelpublishing.com
© 2019 Blind Squirrel Publishing, LLC , All Rights Reserved

BLIND SQUIRREL
PUBLISHING

Deploying a Cloud-hosted environment

How to do it...

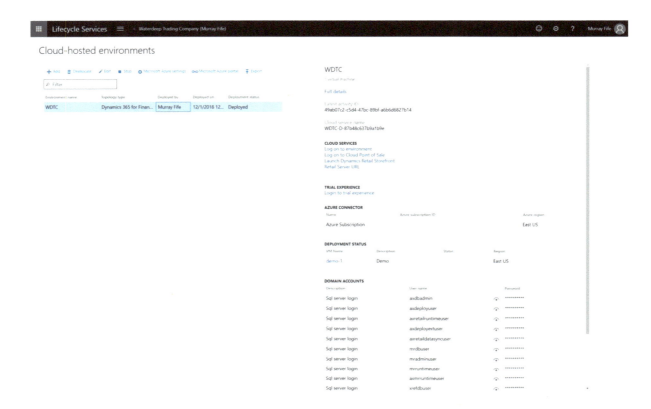

Step 9: Click on the Full details button

This will give us a summary of the Cloud-housed environment with all the access details and links to log into Dynamics 365.

We can see more information about the environment by accessing the full details of the deployment.

To do this all we need to do is click on the **Full details** button.

Deploying a Cloud-hosted environment

How to do it...

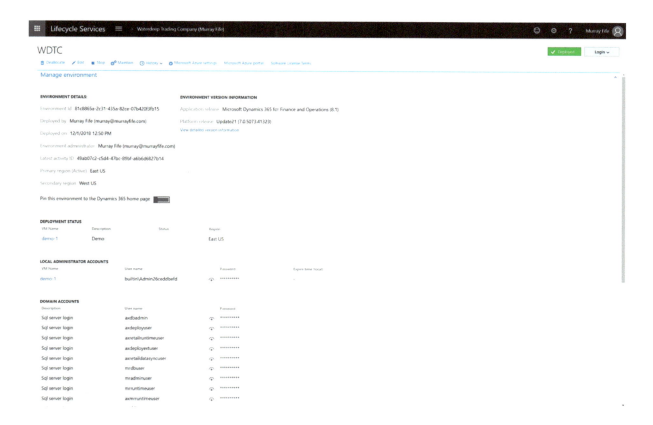

Step 9: Click on the Full details button

This will show us more information about the environment and allow us to maintain the environment by applying patches and updates to. it.

www.dynamicscompanions.com
Dynamics Companions

- 89 -

www.blindsquirrelpublishing.com
© 2019 Blind Squirrel Publishing, LLC , All Rights Reserved

BLIND SQUIRREL
PUBLISHING

Deploying a Cloud-hosted environment

How to do it...

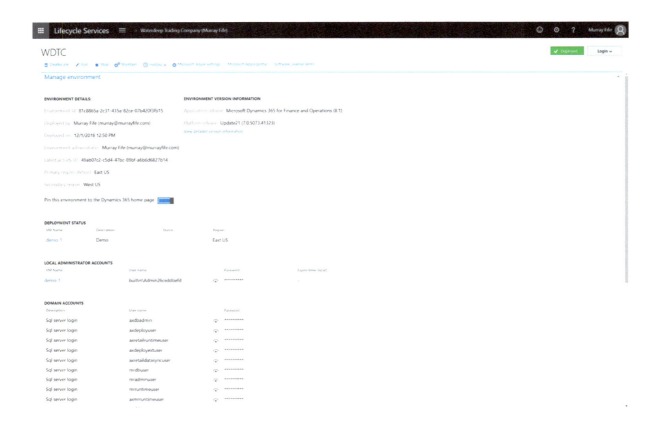

Step 10: Change the Pin this environment to the Dynamics 365 home page

From here we can make a small change which is to add the tile for Dynamics 365 to the home page for Dynamics 365. This is useful because it gives us an easy way to open Dynamics 365.

To do this just switch the Pin this environment to the Dynamics 365 home page value.

For this example, we will want to click on the **Pin this environment to the Dynamics 365 home page** toggle switch and change it to the **Yes** value.

www.dynamicscompanions.com
Dynamics Companions

- 90 -

www.blindsquirrelpublishing.com
© 2019 Blind Squirrel Publishing, LLC , All Rights Reserved

BLIND SQUIRREL
PUBLISHING

Deploying a Cloud-hosted environment

How to do it...

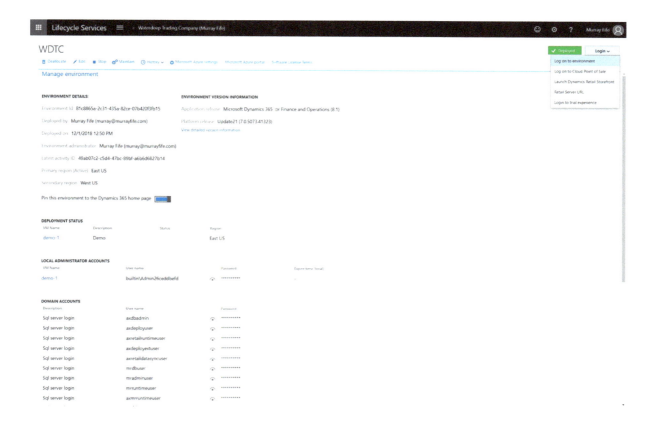

Step 11: Click on the Log on to environment button

Alternatively, we can log on to Dynamics 365 by selecting the Login button in the top right of the page and selecting the way that we want to access the cloud-hosted environment.

To do this just click on the **Log on to environment** button.

www.dynamicscompanions.com
Dynamics Companions

- 91 -

www.blindsquirrelpublishing.com
© 2019 Blind Squirrel Publishing, LLC , All Rights Reserved

BLIND SQUIRREL
PUBLISHING

Opening Dynamics 365 for the first time

Once the **Waterdeep Trading Company** got notification that their **Dynamics 365** instance had been provisioned for them, they wanted to dive in right away and start configuring it right away so that they could keep on their implementation timeline and be up and running before the next surge in sales.

How to do it...

Step 1: Go to home.dynamics.com

Getting into Dynamics 365 was simple. All they needed to do was go to the **Dynamics** home page and then open the home workspace.

Go to home.dynamics.com

Step 2: Click on Dynamics 365 for Finance and Operations tile

To access **Dynamics 365,** they just needed to open the **Finance and Operations** module.

Click on the Dynamics 365 for Finance and Operations tile.

Opening Dynamics 365 for the first time

How to do it...

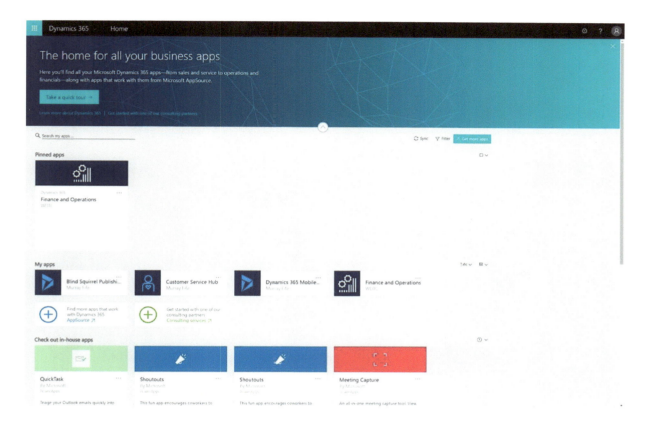

Step 1: Go to home.dynamics.com

Getting into Dynamics 365 was simple. All they needed to do was go to the **Dynamics** home page and then open the home workspace.

To do this they just opened a browser and went to **home.dynamics.com**.

This will take us to the **Dynamics 365** home page where we are able to see all the workloads of Dynamics 365 that they were able to access and there was a tile for **Dynamics 365 for Finance and Operations** which is the core application that they will be setting up.

www.dynamicscompanions.com
Dynamics Companions

- 93 -

www.blindsquirrelpublishing.com
© 2019 Blind Squirrel Publishing, LLC , All Rights Reserved

BLIND SQUIRREL
PUBLISHING

Opening Dynamics 365 for the first time

How to do it...

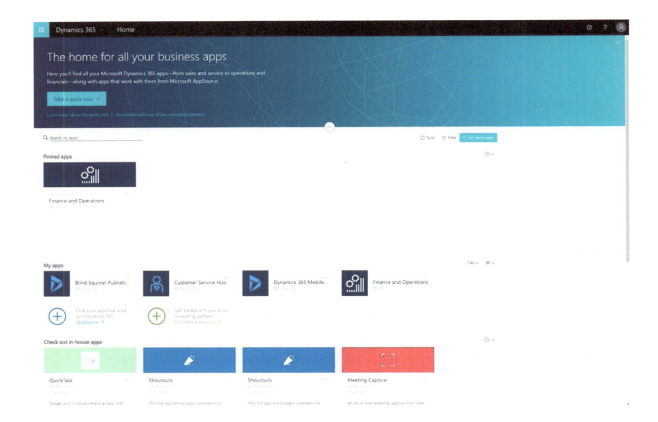

Step 2: Click on Dynamics 365 for Finance and Operations tile

To access **Dynamics 365,** they just needed to open the **Finance and Operations** module.

To do this just click on the Dynamics 365 for Finance and Operations tile.

dync
www.dynamicscompanions.com
Dynamics Companions

- 94 -

www.blindsquirrelpublishing.com
© 2019 Blind Squirrel Publishing, LLC , All Rights Reserved

BLIND SQUIRREL
PUBLISHING

Opening Dynamics 365 for the first time

How to do it...

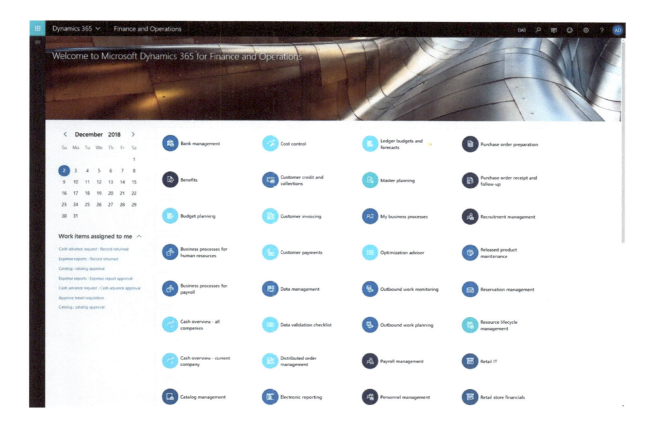

Step 2: Click on Dynamics 365 for Finance and Operations tile

This opens the initial workspace within the **Dynamics 365** module where we see all the different workspaces that are delivered out of the box for them.

dync
www.dynamicscompanions.com
Dynamics Companions

- 95 -

www.blindsquirrelpublishing.com
© 2019 Blind Squirrel Publishing, LLC , All Rights Reserved

BLIND SQUIRREL
PUBLISHING

Review

Getting into **Dynamics 365** was easy for the **Waterdeep Trading Company** administrator, and now that they had access to the full system as the system administrator, they were able to start setting everything up.

Summary

All the hard work is now done. We have a Cloud-hosted environment for Dynamics 365 that we can now start configuring for the **Waterdeep Trading Company.**

The next step is to start setting up the company for them to use.

About The Author

Murray Fife is an Author of over 25 books on Microsoft Dynamics including the Bare Bones Configuration Guide series of over 15 books which step the user through the setup of initial Dynamics instance, then through the Financial modules and then through the configuration of the more specialized modules like production, service management, and project accounting. You can find all his books on Amazon at **www.amazon.com/author/murrayfife**.

For more information on Murray, here is his contact information:

If you are interested in contacting Murray or want to follow his blogs and posts then here is all of his contact information:

Email: murray@murrayfife.com

Twitter: @murrayfife

Facebook: faceook.com/murraycfife

Google: google.com/+murrayfife

LinkedIn: linkedin.com/in/murrayfife

Blog: atinkerersnotebook.com

SlideShare: slideshare.net/murayfife

Amazon: amazon.com/author/murrayfife

dync
www.dynamicscompanions.com
Dynamics Companions

- 98 -

www.blindsquirrelpublishing.com
© 2019 Blind Squirrel Publishing, LLC , All Rights Reserved

BLIND SQUIRREL
PUBLISHING